Quick Tips

in association with

TODAY'S GOLFER *magazine*

SACKVILLE BOOKS

First published in 1990
by Sackville Books Ltd
Stradbroke, Suffolk IP21 5JG England

ISBN 0-948 615-39-7

Designed and produced by Sackville Design Group Ltd
Art Director: Rolando Ugolini
Editor: Mike Henderson

British Library Cataloguing in Publication Data
Golf Quick Tips
1. Golf Techniques — (Sackville Golf Clinic)
I. Today's Golfer
796 3523

Typeset by Jean Cussons, Diss, Norfolk, England
Printed and bound in Italy by New Interlitho SPA, Milan.

Quick Tips

Contents

Introduction

Faced with unexpected or reoccuring problems in his or her game, the average golfer can turn to the local professional for advice, which may be expensive and time-consuming. In many cases however, it is simple and easy to diagnose the problem yourself and cure the fault.

This collection of Quick Tips is an invaluable aid for the average golfer, offering over sixty useful hints to overcoming the most common and recurrent difficulties of the game. How do you correct a slice? What are the special grips for putting? How far should you stand from the ball at the address? How do you get the maximum distance on your shots? How do you cure lazy leg action? All aspects of the game are covered from the tee to the green. The tips have been written as concisely and straight-forwardly as possible, in a non-technical way, and besides curing faults, will offer many new ideas for generally improving your play.

CHAPTER 1

The address

Finding the right position

Many club golfers find difficulty in deciding just how far they should stand from the ball at address. However, there is a simple rule-of-thumb routine you can follow which might help solve that problem.

First of all, standing with your feet apart, hold the club fully extended, straight out in front of you. Then, bend from the waist until the clubhead lies flat on the turf. Finally, slightly flex the knees to complete the drill.

This simple exercise will put you the correct distance from the ball at address across the range of clubs from driver to sand wedge.

Clap hands

Check your hand position. The left hand and right hand positions will be aligned this way if you have gripped the club correctly. They must be returned to this position of alignment at the point of impact.

Some golfers fail to grasp this basic requirement and therefore develop the wrong type of hand action. Their grip to alleviate an error in wrist action results in some grips looking as if they belong in a horror movie.

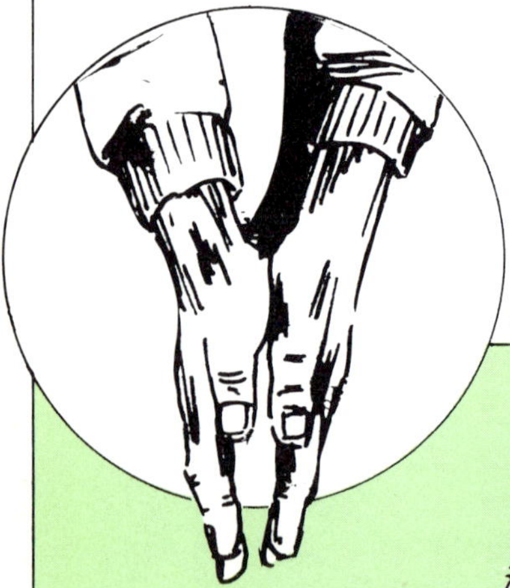

Sitting down

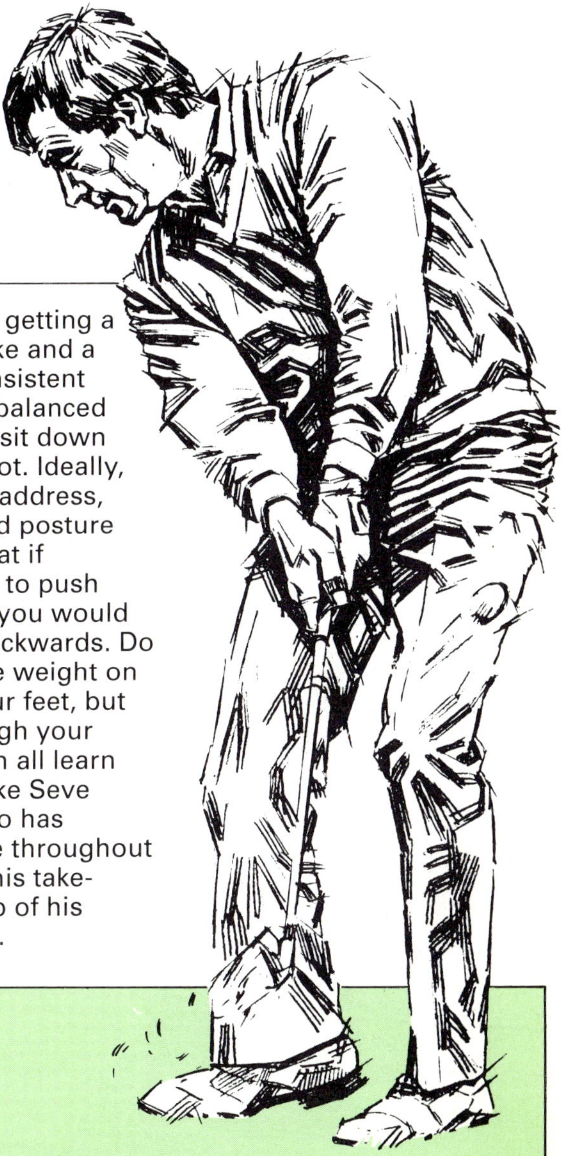

The key to getting a solid strike and a more consistent swing is to be balanced and to literally sit down through the shot. Ideally, you should, at address, have such good posture and balance that if someone were to push your forehead you would not fall over backwards. Do not have all the weight on the balls of your feet, but spread it through your insteps. We can all learn from players like Seve Ballesteros who has perfect balance throughout the shot from his take-away to the top of his follow-through.

Do not ground the driver head

You may have noticed that some of the top players in the game such as Jack Nicklaus, Bernhard Langer and Sam Torrance, to mention only three, do not ground the driver head when they address the ball but instead hold it fractionally in the air.

These top players practise this method to help avoid tension building up in the hands and forearms. When the club is grounded the player is tending to press downwards and in so doing creates a muscular resistance that leads to tension in the hands and arms. A chain reaction passes through the rest of the body.

A second reason to keep the club fractionally above the ground is that it prevents the clubhead touching any protruding earth and turf that could throw the club off line.

Perhaps most importantly, holding the club slightly above the ground helps all parts of the body involved in the takeaway to act smoothly as one unit — instead of each part working independently and then having to come together in the downswing.

If you do adopt this method try it out on the practice ground before you enter any competition.

All the top golfers hold the club above the grass if they are playing from the rough. This is because, should they ground the club in the grass behind the ball and the ball moves, they would incur a penalty stroke.

CHAPTER 2

The swing

Curing a slice

If you make a good weight transference but still keep slicing the ball, the fault could lie in you getting ahead of the ball at impact. In that position the hands cannot release properly.

One way to prevent getting ahead of yourself is to make a concerted effort to focus on the back of the ball and put more emphasis on the arm swing and less your leg action.

A simple practice pointer is to hit balls with your feet together and this will help you to further understand the role of your hands and arms.

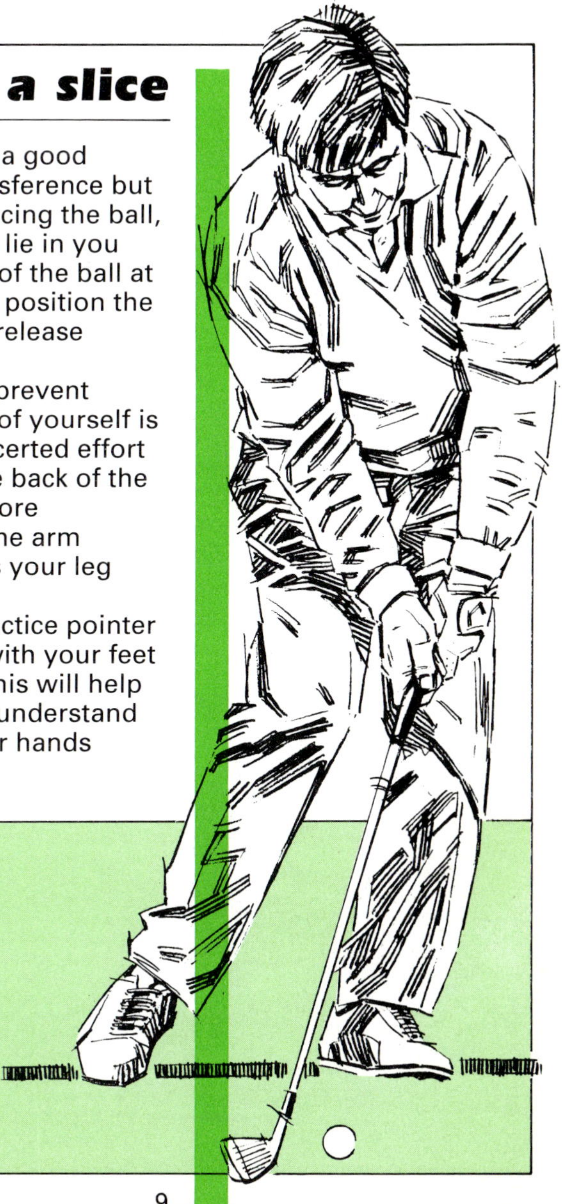

The waggle — full swing to miniature

Watch the majority of handicap golfers and it is apparent that the term waggle is not in their golfing dictionary. Most approach the ball in a haphazard manner and then hit it without thinking. The waggle would benefit all golfers as it programmes the real swing.

Next time you play a round of golf, as you stand over the ball, look at the target and, as the shot forms in your imagination, allow your hands to move the club back and forth over the ball in the manner you intend to hit it.

If you need to hit the ball a long way with the driver, say into a strong headwind or over water, then waggle the club a little quicker and with conviction. If on the other hand, you intend to hit a nice, smooth 7 iron to the green, then waggle the club slowly, smoothly and much more deliberately than normal. In a bunker when you need to slide the sand wedge under the ball on an out-to-in path, waggle the club back from the ball on the angle that you intend the club to enter the sand.

In short, the waggle is the full swing in miniature. It also loosens up the muscles before the swing commences. However, look at it as a way of establishing in your mind the path on which the clubhead is going to travel and the tempo of the swing. Remember, do not just move the clubhead to loosen up, waggle the club as you intend to hit the shot and watch your scores fall.

Tune into the Triangle Method

If you have problems making a good shoulder turn, try the Triangle Method. This swing triangle is formed by the hands at the bottom and the shoulders at the top forming an inverted triangle shape. The idea is

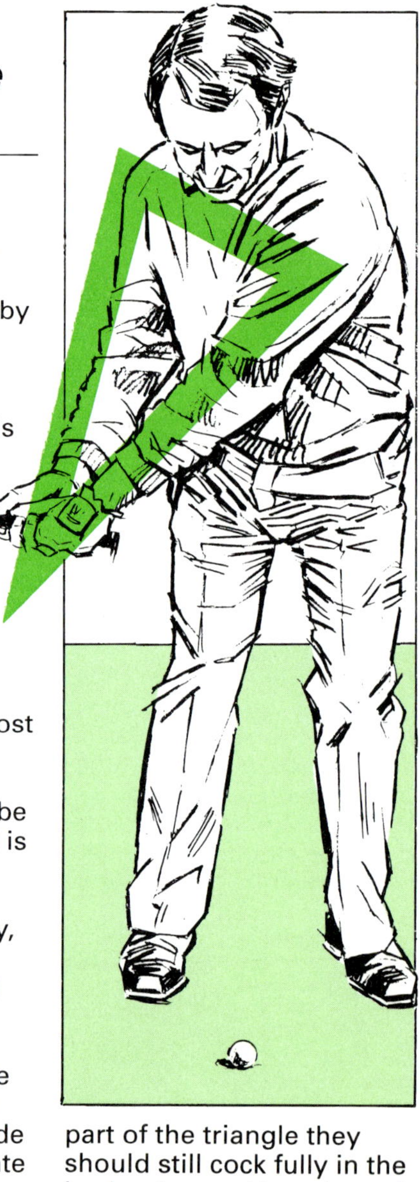

that shoulders and hands work in unison, taking the club back, and it should be possible when making a full swing, to retain that triangle relationship almost throughout the whole of the swing.

The first advantage to be gained from this method is that it helps to start the backswing with a one-piece takeaway. Secondly, it encourages the left shoulder to make a good turn under the chin and helps you to get your hands as high as possible in the backswing. This in turn provides a good, wide arc from which to generate power and distance.

A word of caution. The hands must not become dead in the swing. Although the hands are a part of the triangle they should still cock fully in the backswing and be released through the hitting area, provided that they remain on a plane with the rest of the swing.

Full turn

Most major faults in golf stem from poor shoulder turn. The two main problems are tilting the shoulders instead of turning them, and turning with the left shoulder and not the right, so that the left arm is pulled across the chest.

The first objective of full shoulder turn is accuracy and the second is distance. The less you turn your shoulders and hips on the backswing, the more U-shaped and upright your swing will be, and consequently the less chance you will have of making a solid strike, or getting any further than the edge of the tee box.

Concentrating on turning the right shoulder will help you turn both shoulders completely.

Shooting from the hip

Lifting the right hip in the backswing, Mae West style, is a guarantee of inconsistency because this kind of movement blocks the action of the arms, causing the upper body to over react and the left side to collapse towards the ball. The result is usually seen as an overswing and no amount of tips or hints will produce a consistent strike from such a position.

The correct body position, as seen in most top class golfers, is the hallmark of a good swing. Conversely, the 'Mae West' action is the opposite. Compare our two illustrations, noting particularly the angle of the back.

Most golfers fall into the 'Mae West' trap because they lift the club too steeply in the backswing. This causes the

The 'Mae West' trap

left shoulder to dip down towards the ball and forces the right hip up above the height of the left.

To cure this fault you should concentrate on turning the shoulders on a level plane. This will not only help to cure the problem, but to encourage a much wider swinging arc which in turn will promote more consistent striking and create a source of additional power.

The correct body position

Quick Tips

Brace your right leg for balance

If you swing too fast then problems of balance arise. What happens is that during the upswing as the weight is naturally transferred onto the right foot, the weight goes too far to the right, buckling the right ankle. You lose both balance and the chance of making an effective swing. By bracing the right leg you can concentrate your weight on the inside of the right foot to maintain your balance before the downswing and transfer of weight to your left foot.

The alignment of the right foot at the finish of the swing can reveal a lot about the swing itself. If your right foot is roughly vertical after you have gone up onto its toes, it is likely that you have swung correctly.

The pitfalls of the flying right elbow

The flying right elbow has always been called a swing fault. The purists will tell us that the right elbow must point towards the ground in both the backswing and the downswing.

Well, Jack Nicklaus, Eamonn Darcy and one of our brightest new amateur stars, Russell Claydon, use this so-called fault to good effect.

They 'fly the right elbow' on the backswing but then bring it back into position in the downswing.

However, it is best to follow the purist and point the right elbow towards the ground. For unless you have the natural talent and feel of the three players mentioned, the flying right elbow will usually lead to a slice.

Tip from Brian Waites, professional, Hollinwell GC, England

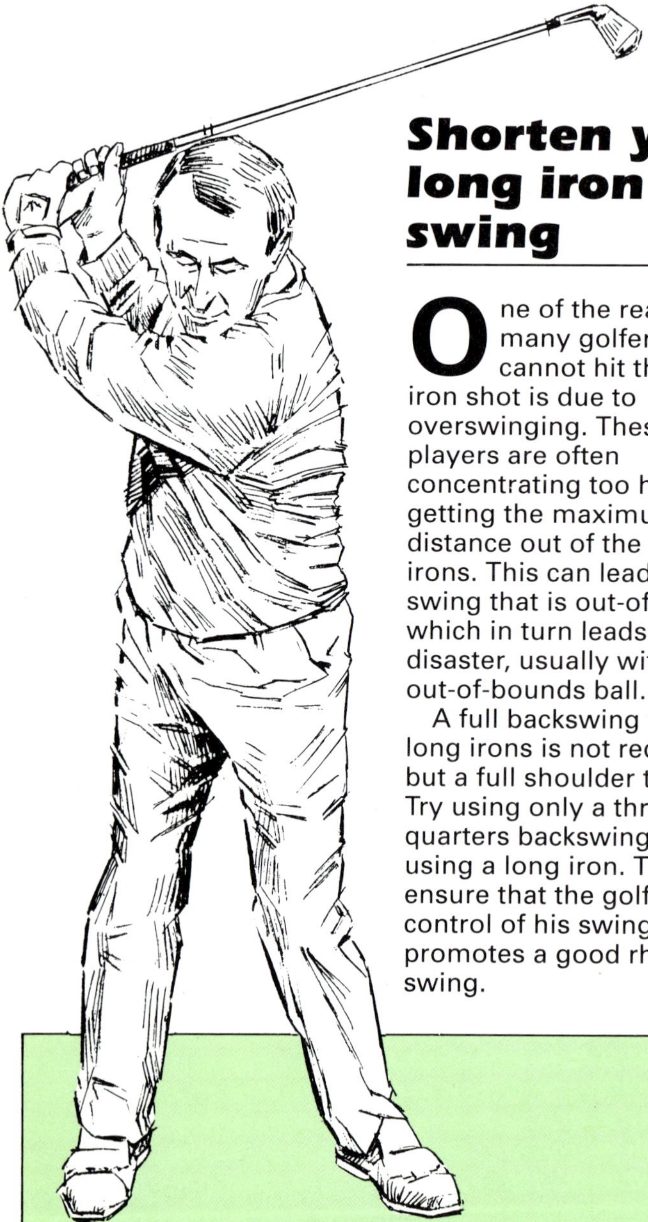

Shorten your long iron swing

One of the reasons so many golfers cannot hit the long iron shot is due to overswinging. These players are often concentrating too hard on getting the maximum distance out of the long irons. This can lead to a swing that is out-of-control which in turn leads to disaster, usually with an out-of-bounds ball.

A full backswing with the long irons is not required, but a full shoulder turn is. Try using only a three-quarters backswing when using a long iron. This will ensure that the golfer is in control of his swing. It also promotes a good rhythmic swing.

Making a good shoulder turn

One way of making a good winding action is to try to ensure that your left knee gets to a position in the backswing where it points behind rather than directly at the ball.

This movement will help you to remember to try to make the best turn you can and at the same time will ensure that you transfer your weight correctly to your right side.

Starting back

The key to a good swing has to start in the takeaway and the backswing that follows, but so much is written about the theory of the backswing that it is easy for the club golfers to become confused.

As Bobby Jones once said: "To watch a man start his backswing is an infallible indication of his worth as a golfer."

So try to concentrate on swinging your hands and arms around and up on a more upright plane than your shoulders. It is important to have a clear picture in your mind of the actual shape of the backswing in relation to the body.

Various teachers use different images but one that has worked well through the years is the image of the swing plane as the plane of glass resting on the shoulders in a line down to the ball.

Having got a precise picture in our mind of the *line* of the backswing, then fix on being smooth and rhythmic.

Pulling the bell rope

Professional golfers often like to have a key thought which will help them to initiate the downswing. Ben Hogan, for instance, felt that the turning of the hips back to the left began the downswing. One of the most common start-down thoughts on the Tour is to imagine that you are pulling a bell rope. In other words, pull down with the left arm.

As long as your left arm does not bend as it pulls, and as long as your legs work ahead of your arms, then that is an excellent method. Beware of swinging with your arms alone because your right shoulder will move forward and you will come over the top of the ball.

Tip from Brian Waites, Hollinwell GC, England

Quick Tips

Keeping the left arm straight in the downswing

Keeping the left arm straight throughout the swing may be an admirable goal, but the handicap golfer often finds it difficult to achieve.

One man who certainly made his mark promoting the straight left arm action is Gary Player. However, few weekend golfers will ever be able to match the little South African's strength and suppleness: assets which are essential when playing this way.

Nevertheless, there are advantages to be gained from a straight left arm, especially in the downswing. Firstly it helps prevent the arm bending in a 'chopping' action that robs the swing of power. A straight left arm on the way down will also give you a wide arc and help to produce maximum power and speed at impact.

So if you cannot match Gary Player's swing to the top of the backswing, do not worry, because you can still cash in on the benefits of keeping the left arm straight in the downswing.

Get high by staying down

One of the weekend golfer's most common faults is lifting the head too soon after impact. What in fact happens is that the player, too eager to see the results of this shot, lifts up his or her head before impact.

This error often results in a topped shot because as the head comes up so does the body and in turn the arc of the swing.

In this picture American star Ben Crenshaw demonstrates the classic follow-through position. The ball is long gone but Gentle Ben has still kept his head in the perfect position well into his follow through.

Rotate the arms on the through swing

Many golfers never attain the full distance on their shots because they do not rotate the arms in the through swing.

Just as arms rotate on the back swing, with the right arm folding in at the side, the arms also rotate on the through swing. As the hands release through the ball, the right hand turns over the left, with the left arm eventually folding on the follow through.

At the 3 o'clock position, the clubhead should be pointing straight at the target, the weight should be on the left foot and the right hand should be on top of the left.

A good thought to have in the through swing is of trying to touch the left forearm with the right. You won't actually achieve this feat, but it's a good image to have during the swing.

So rotate those arms in the through swing and you will soon be adding yards to your drives.

Feet first

A common problem for amateur golfers is failing to clear the left side properly in the throughswing, especially when it comes to the woods and long irons. It is a fault that can lead to several swing errors, including slicing, pushing and even in some cases skying.

The fault can often be traced not to the swing but to the position of the feet.

Many amateur golfers fall into the trap of positioning both feet at right angles to the target line when they address the ball. By slightly opening the left foot, it encourages the body to move freely through the shot, creating more power and subsequently, better and longer shots.

When the left foot is positioned square instead of slightly open it can act as a barrier to proper weight transfer and leads to differing swing errors.

Finding the right direction

When it comes to direction problems, the faulty position of the left wrist at the top of the backswing is often to blame.

Picture (A) shows the ideal position from which to produce a square hit with the back of the left wrist, the hand and the full arm all forming a straight line and all on the same plane.

Picture (B) is known as the 'arched' position and usually leads to the clubface being returned to the ball in a closed position, resulting in a hooked shot.

Picture (C) shows the wrists in a cupped or open position, common to many amateur golfers and which could lead to a slice.

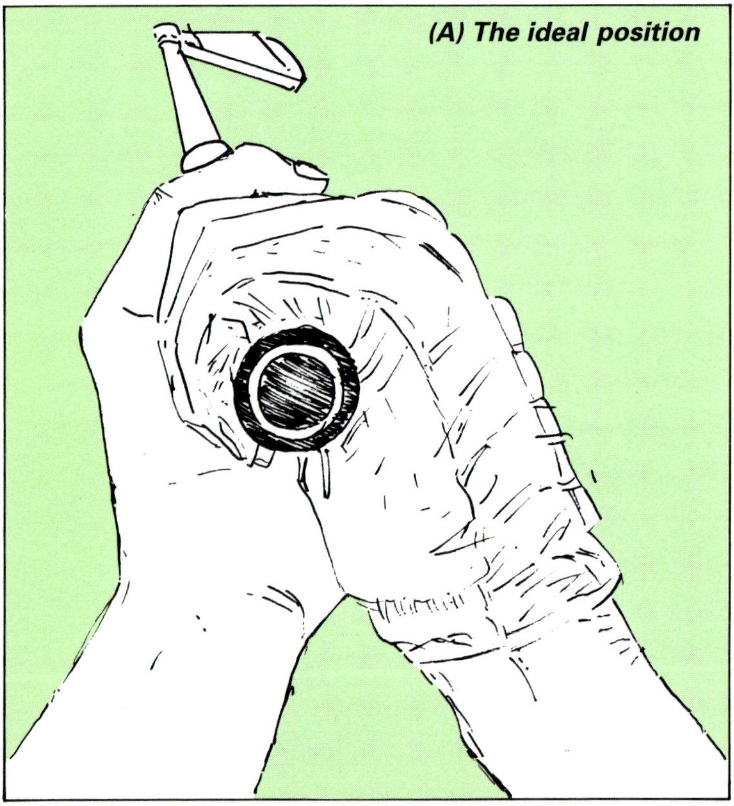

(A) The ideal position

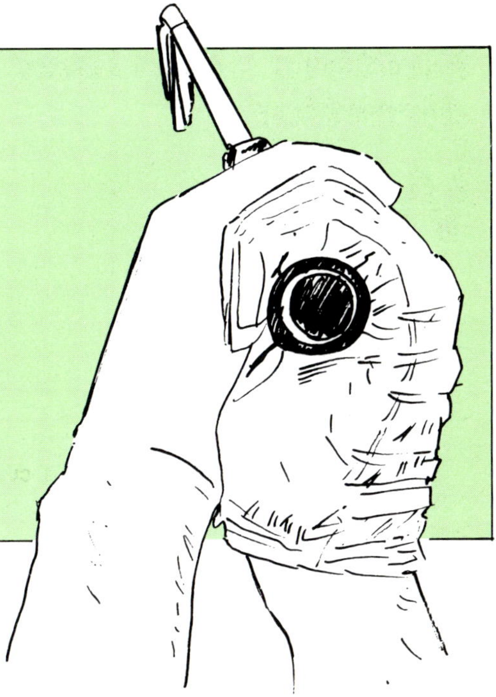

(B) The 'arched' position

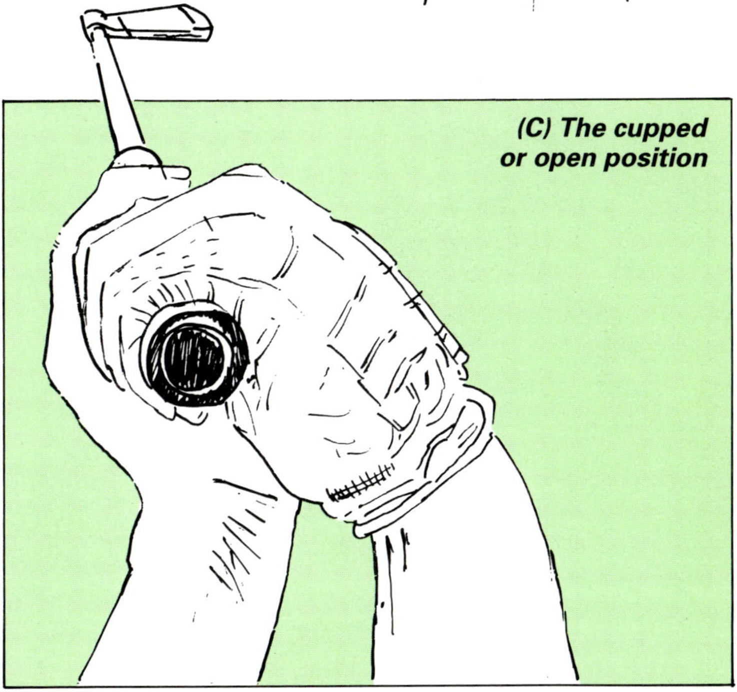

(C) The cupped or open position

Keep your head back

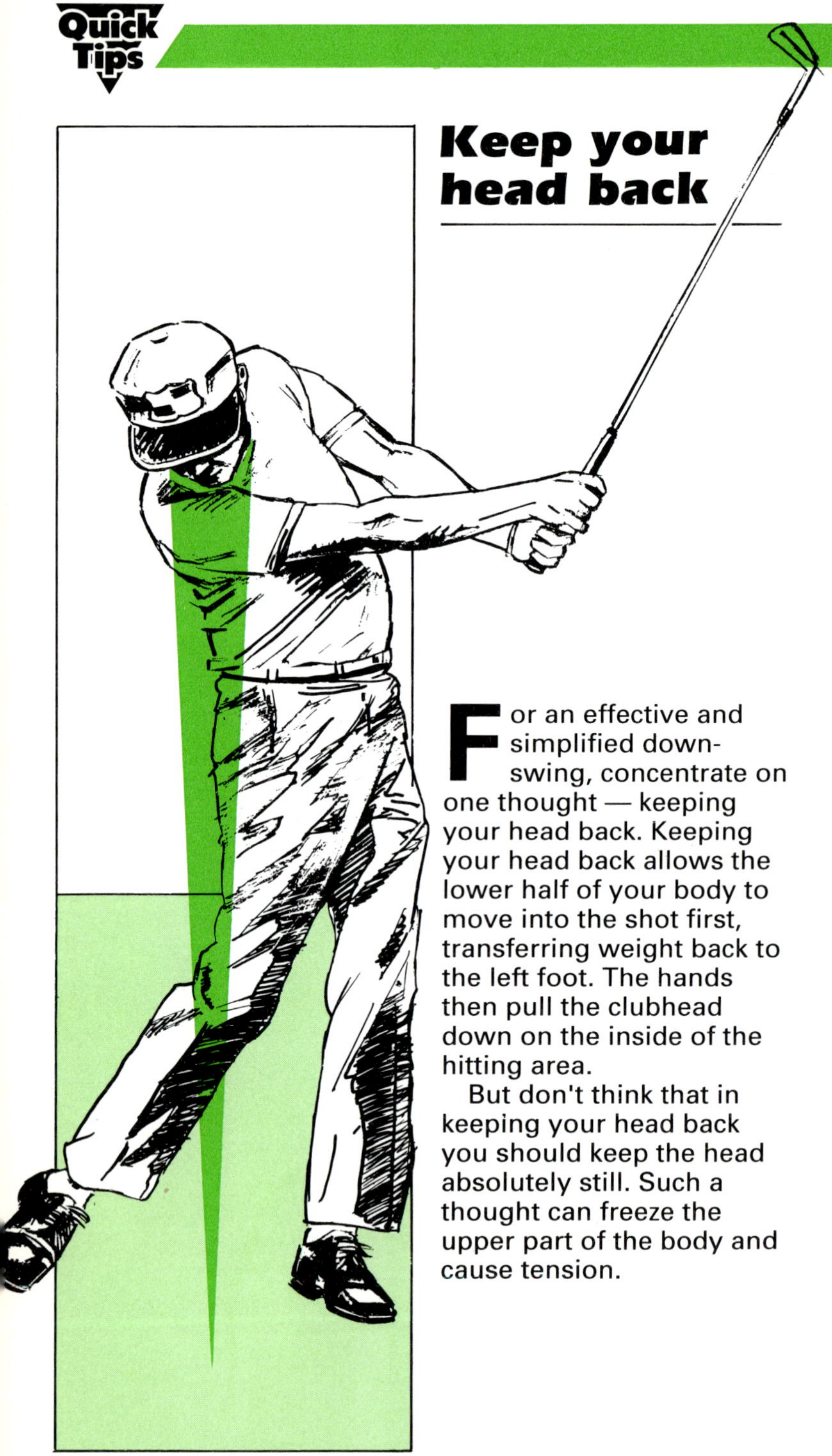

For an effective and simplified downswing, concentrate on one thought — keeping your head back. Keeping your head back allows the lower half of your body to move into the shot first, transferring weight back to the left foot. The hands then pull the clubhead down on the inside of the hitting area.

But don't think that in keeping your head back you should keep the head absolutely still. Such a thought can freeze the upper part of the body and cause tension.

Beat the slice

Hitting from the top encourages the right shoulder to dominate the downswing and can lead to a slice. To prevent the right shoulder coming in too soon, as you address the ball concentrate on the image of your belt buckle facing directly towards the target as you swing through to a full follow-through position. Concentrating on the buckle will certainly help you to make the lower half of your body the dominant factor in the downswing.

The widest possible arc

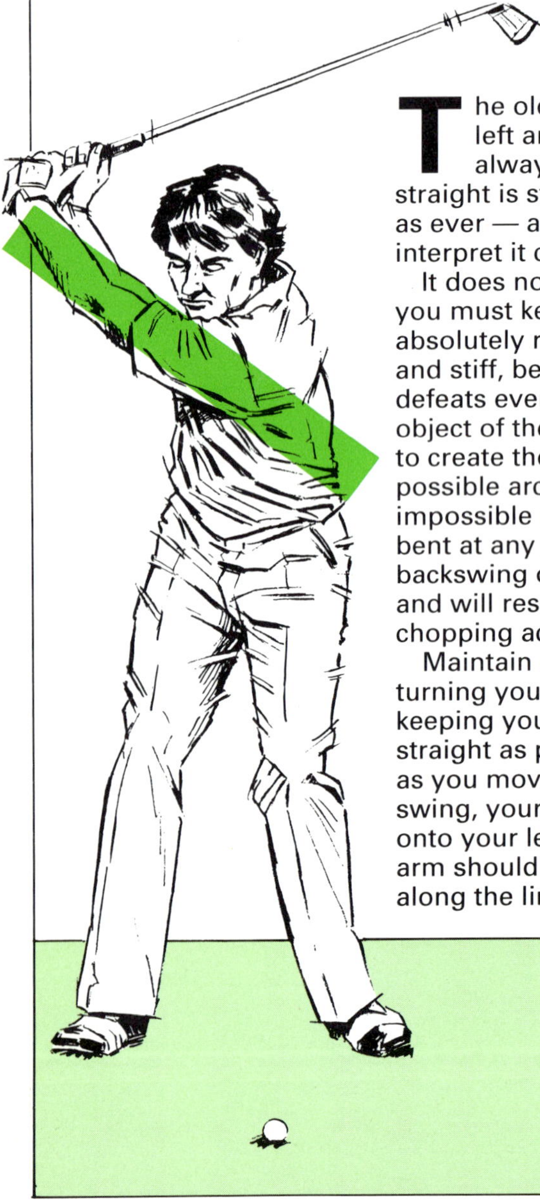

The old adage that the left arm should always be kept straight is still as relevant as ever — as long as you interpret it correctly.

It does not mean that you must keep the arm absolutely ramrod straight and stiff, because that defeats everything. The object of the golf swing is to create the widest possible arc. That is impossible if the left arm is bent at any point in the backswing or downswing, and will result in a chopping action.

Maintain a wide arc by turning your shoulders and keeping your left arm as straight as possible. Then as you move into the down swing, your weight shifts onto your left leg and your arm should be pulling along the line of the shaft.

Chin up

If, concentrating on the swing, you allow your head to drop against your chest, you will find it virtually impossible to start the club back along the correct path. A further fault that arises is that by blocking the natural path of your shoulders and arms in the backswing, you will be forced to pick up the club far too steeply.

This will not only lead to chopping down on the ball in the downswing but will also deprive the backswing of any width and result in a lack of power in your shots.

Pull the handle

If your right shoulder comes over the top on the downswing, the clubhead will travel along an out-to-in swing path and a sliced shot will result.

To restrain this destructive shoulder action, concentrate on pulling the butt, or end, of the handle of the club, down towards the ball in the downswing. This will make you more left arm conscious and will encourage the right elbow to stay close to the body in the downswing. The clubhead should now travel on an in-to-out swing path.

Turn, don't tilt

Overswinging can be more harmful than swinging short but unfortunately it is difficult to gauge the length of your backswing. Many golfers fool themselves into believing that they are making a full shoulder turn when they are tilting rather than turning. If the left heel rises up and this combines with too narrow a stance and a tilting shoulder, it is a recipe for disaster. A narrow stance also fails to encourage the proper winding or coiling action.

If you suffer from overswinging, try widening your stance. This will make it more difficult to swing the club past the horizontal in the backswing. There is nothing wrong with a short backswing, provided that it is accompanied by a proper shoulder turn which fully winds the muscles.

Quick Tips

Let the left heel act naturally

Too many golfers seem to think that good golf rests with how they use their left heel in the backswing. Watch your playing partners the next time you're playing and concentrate on how they use their left heel. Many deliberately lift the left heel because they have seen the greats, Jack Nicklaus for example, lift it off the ground. Others try to keep the left heel on the ground at all costs, which usually results in all the weight being thrown to the left on the backswing.

The truth is that the great golfers don't worry about what their left heel is doing in the backswing. The left heel is simply a reaction to the full swing. Ben Hogan, for example, never thought about what his left foot was doing in the backswing.

Whether or not the left heel comes off the ground depends on the body and leg action involved in the backswing. As long as you ensure that the weight coils around the right leg on the back swing, then you don't need to worry about what your left heel is doing; it simply follows as the last action of the backswing and becomes the first action of the downswing as the body completes its turn and then the hips turn to initiate the downswing.

So remember, don't worry about the left heel. If it comes off the ground, fine, and if it stays rooted to the ground then so be it.

Getting it together

If the start to your backswing is becoming disjointed, perhaps by thinking too much about different aspects of the swing, try these two swing triggers.

The first is the 'Forward Press'. Take up your normal address position with your hands level with the ball. Now press your hands slightly to the left and start the club back. This seems to help gather together swing components such as weight transfer and shoulder turn.

For the second trigger start the backswing by 'kicking' the right knee towards the target. Once again take up your normal position but now, instead of starting the club straight back with the hands and arms, press the right knee towards the target. Then almost as a rebounding action, the right leg moves back to the right and acts as a key to stimulating the other components of the backswing into synchronized action.

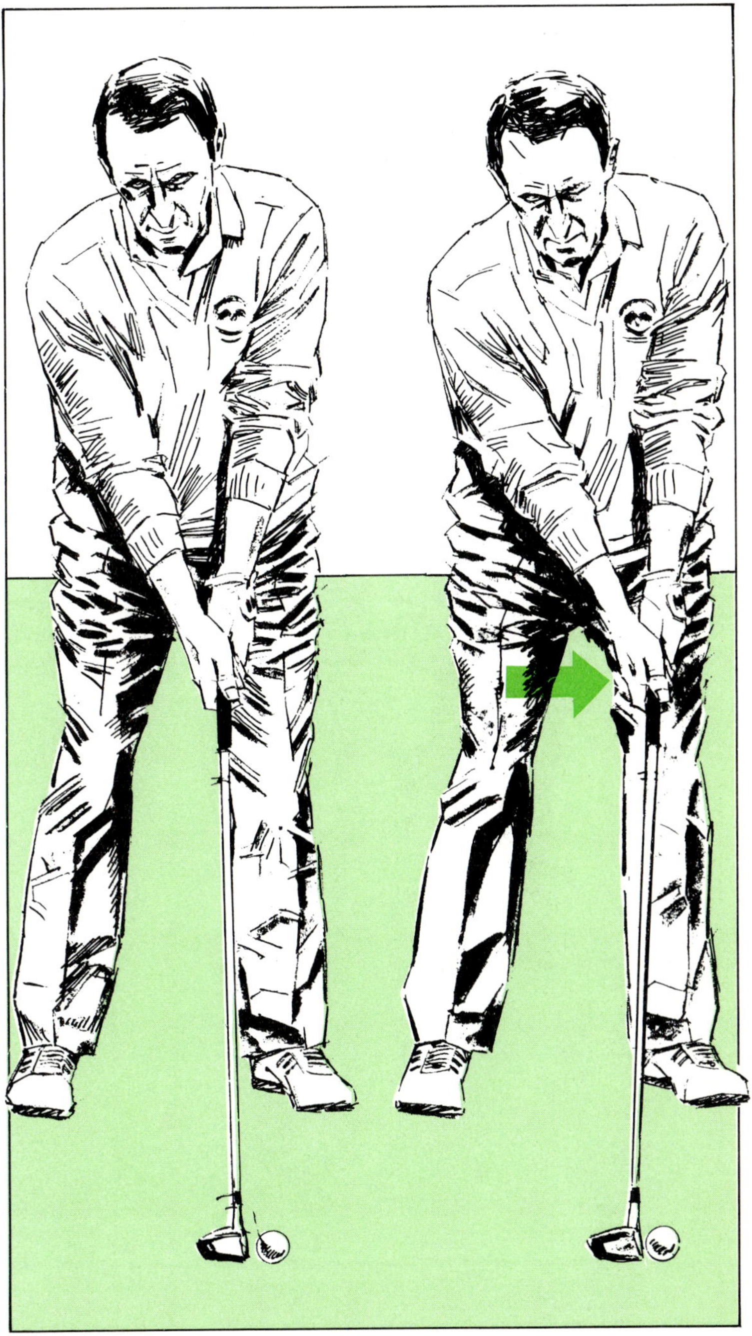

Stop coming over the top

The term coming over the top may be foreign to many players, but it is something amateur players do quite often. Essentially the term refers to a downswing which is initiated by the shoulders rather than the legs.

It is almost impossible to play good golf when you begin the downswing with the shoulders. A downswing which begins with the shoulders results in an out-to-in swing path. This causes the dreaded slice if the clubface is open at impact, a pulled shot left of the target if the clubface is square and a pull-hook should the clubface be closed.

At the top of the swing you should resist the temptation to throw the club with the shoulders. Try to feel the legs and hips turning back towards the target. The shoulders and arms simply follow the turning of the lower body.

Here is a good exercise to get the true feeling of how the downswing begins. Take the club to the top of the backswing and then turn the hips back to the left. By doing this you will notice that the top of the body is turned back towards the target and the arms have been pulled down towards the ball.

Curing lazy leg action

One of the most common faults of amateur golfers is lazy leg action and subsequently bad co-ordination between the upper body and the lower body through the swing. Starting down using only your shoulders and the upper half of your body will tend to make you hit from the top, and either block the ball out to the right or snap hook.

A good rule is to concentrate on turning the upper body on the backswing, allowing the hips to remain passive, and to move your hips and legs in the downswing allowing your hands and arms to follow. Starting down correctly by using the legs is the key to an ideal swing path (in-to-out) and to a powerful hitting action. Some players, such as Sam Torrance, think of slamming the left heel back to earth, while others, such as Ben Hogan turn the hips.

Lifting the right heel early on the downswing encourages good leg action and clears the hips, promoting a powerful in-to-out action through the ball.

CHAPTER 3

Driving

The low down of driving

If you are having problems with your driver, especially chopping down on the ball, try to consciously keep the driver low to the ground during the first 12 inches of the backswing.

This will help produce a wider and therefore shallower arc which in the downswing, will prevent you coming down too sharply on the ball and ballooning it straight up into the air. With a flatter swing plane you should meet the ball more on the upswing, which is the ideal line to get the best results from your driver.

Shortening your grip for straighter driving

One of the main reasons why weekend golfers have trouble with the driver is because it is the longest club in the bag.

The further they have to stand from the ball, the less confident they feel. This, coupled with the fact that the driver is usually the cause of more dropped shots than any other club does not exactly help to instill a feeling of confidence.

One way to overcome the problem and produce more accurate tee shots with the driver is to get yourself close to the ball by holding the club further down the handle than normal.

This will obviously mean adjusting the distance that you stand from the ball and although you may lose a few yards in length, you will probably find that you will hit a lot more fairways.

Improved accuracy will result from your shortened grip.

Shoulder through the ball

To hit golf balls long distances it is vital to drive the right shoulder 'through the ball' and end with a follow-through with the hands finishing high. The swing begins with the left shoulder, left hand and clubhead going back in one piece. It is important to remember that on the downswing the left shoulder should, if possible, turn as much as 180 degrees.

To help make this happen you must drive the right shoulder through the ball and follow through until the hands are high.

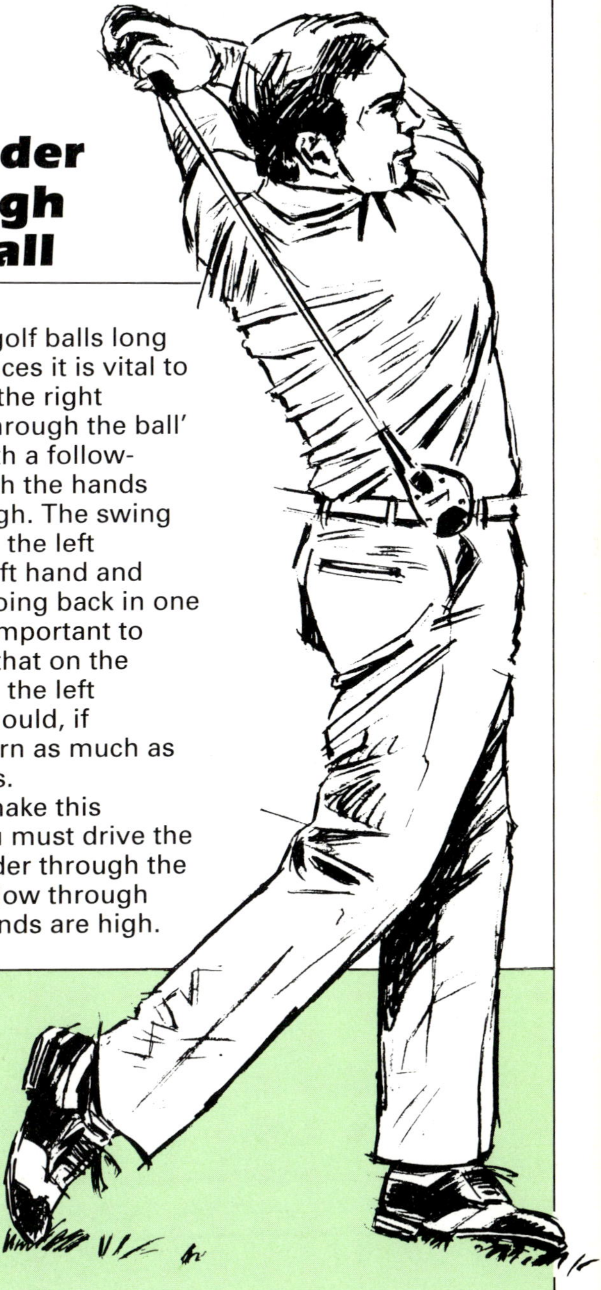

CHAPTER 4

The fairway

Beat the wet with woods

Winter invariably brings wetness as well as cold and there are many occasions when the fairways become damp and soggy. When playing long shots from the fairway in these conditions, try using a fairway wood instead of an iron. If you play a long iron in wet conditions, water tends to get between the ball and the club face, reducing the amount of spin imparted.

Because it is spinning less, the ball will not get airborne as easily as in the dry. With a fairway wood, the sweeping action makes it easier to get the ball up and away.

Focus on the back of the ball

One of the sweetest shots in golf is a well struck shot off the fairway using a wood, but often a tight lie will foil even the best of golfers.

The main point to remember with this shot is to make sure you stay down on it for as long as possible and one tip which has worked for many golfers is to concentrate on the back of the ball.

By focusing on the back of the ball, or even the logo, you tend not to lift up on the shot and are more likely to extend through and along the target line.

Up and away

Many high handicappers are advised to use fairway woods in preference to long irons because it is generally easier to get the ball airborne with the woods.

In most instances this is sound advice. However, it is essential to make sure when playing a fairway wood that the ball is positioned correctly in the stance.

Some golfers believe that all the woods should be played with the ball positioned opposite the left heel, and maintain this ball position from the driver, right through to the 5, or even, the 7 wood.

Although opposite the left heel may be the ideal for the driver, it can be a different story when it comes to the fairway woods and in many instances playing the ball too far forward in the stance can lead to topping shots.

If you suffer from this problem, try moving the ball back slightly towards the middle of your stance, as you cannot bring the full loft of the clubface onto the ball unless the ball is positioned to make contact at the lowest point of the club's arc.

The middle irons

One advantage with middle irons is that there is no reason for the weekend golfer to hit these clubs hard. If more distance is required, simply take more club, and keep the same tempo.

The address position is very important. Position the ball just left of centre in the stance, which should be square, or slightly open. Position the hands far enough ahead of the clubface to ensure that the shaft of the club and the left arm form a straight line, when viewed from the front of the player. With the hands in this position, the grip can be assumed at the right angle.

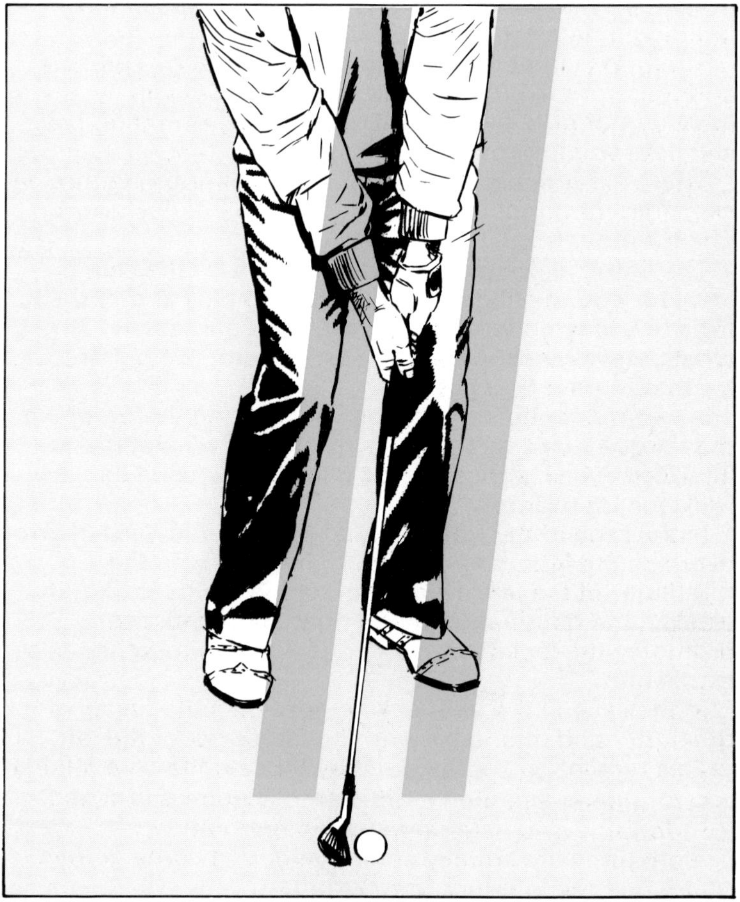

CHAPTER 5

Grips

Grip choice

If you get the chance to watch the top players in action you will probably notice that they all have their own individual way of swinging the golf club.

However, the one thing that all these top stars have in common is a good grip. If you do not have a sound grip you will never be able to realise your full potential as a golfer and that is why it is one of the main factors in building a better game.

The grip is important because it controls the clubface and therefore the direction in which the ball will fly; if you have a poor grip, no amount of practice just hitting balls will help you improve.

There are three acceptable methods of gripping the club: The Vardon, or orthodox grip; The Interlock; and The Hammer grip.

The latter, which places all ten fingers on the club is ideal for young children just starting to play and perhaps for a few lady golfers who do not have particularly strong wrists. However, it is seldom seen among pro golfers, or for that matter, club golfers.

The two most popular methods of gripping therefore are the Vardon (used by the majority of golfers) and the Interlock, which although less common, is used by Jack Nicklaus for example.

In the case of the right-handed players, the Vardon grip overlaps the little finger of the right hand with the forefinger of the left. This 'overlapping' helps to slightly weaken the domination of the right hand and also promotes the feeling of the hands working together as a single unit.

In the case of the Interlocking grip, the little finger of the right hand interlocks with the forefinger of the left.

This type of grip is favoured by those golfers with fairly short fingers, who find it difficult to acquire a firm and comfortable grip using the Vardon method.

Both grips are equally correct although some golfers claim that the Interlock grip permits.

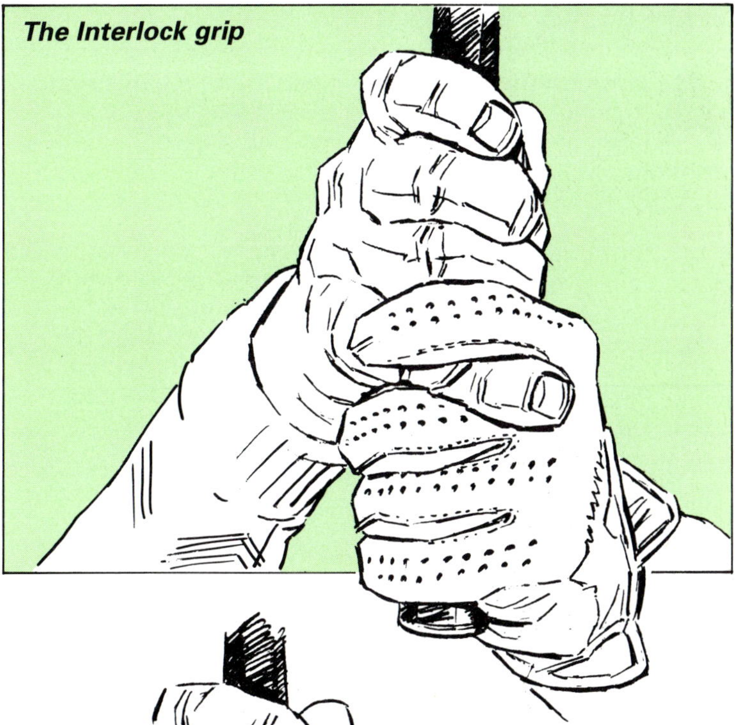

The Interlock grip

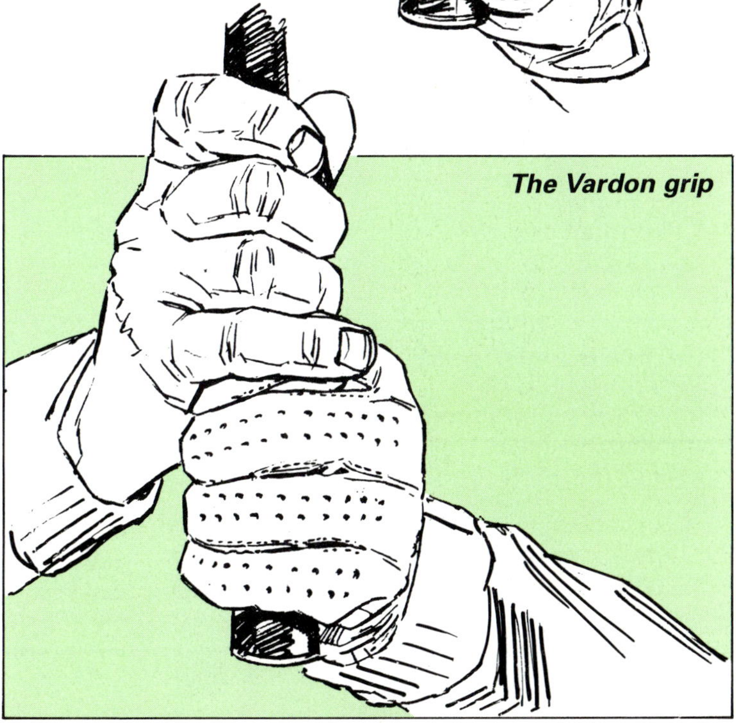

The Vardon grip

Putting Grips

Although there are three basic models of gripping the club, when it comes to gripping the putter, almost anything goes, provided it gets the ball in the hole.

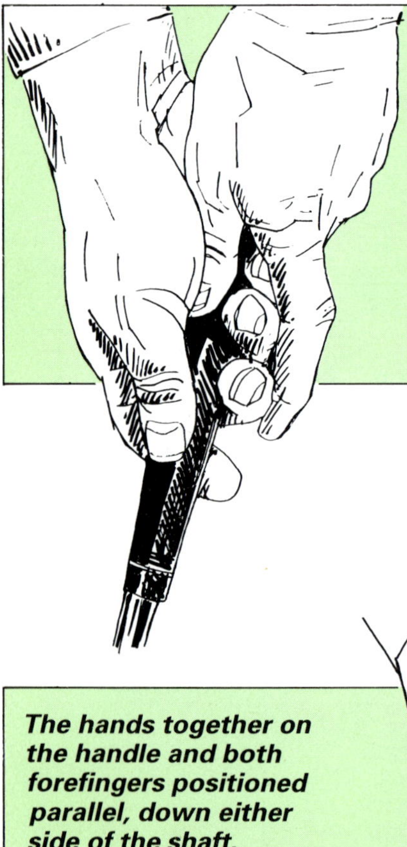

The most common putting grip with the index finger of the left hand overlapping the fingers of the right hand.

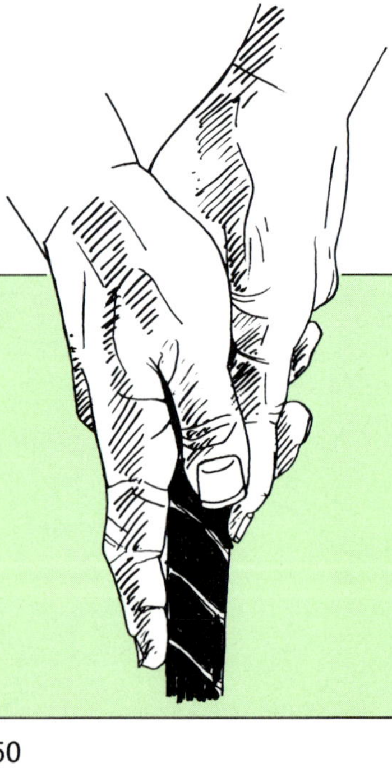

The hands together on the handle and both forefingers positioned parallel, down either side of the shaft.

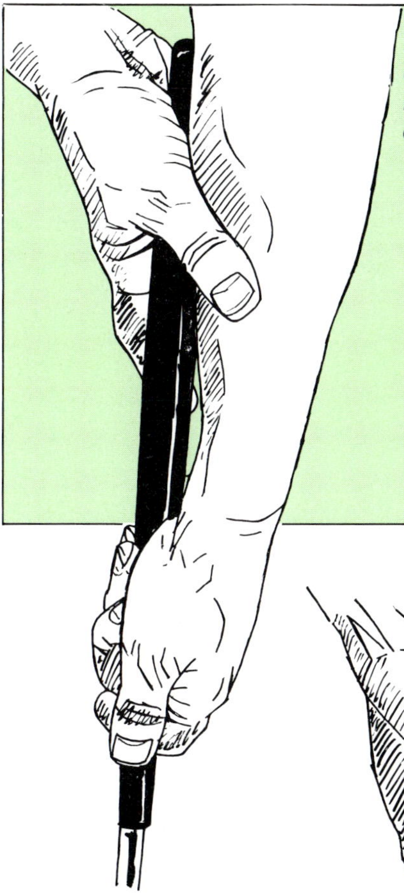

This type of grip is designed to take any hand or wrist action out of the putting stroke.

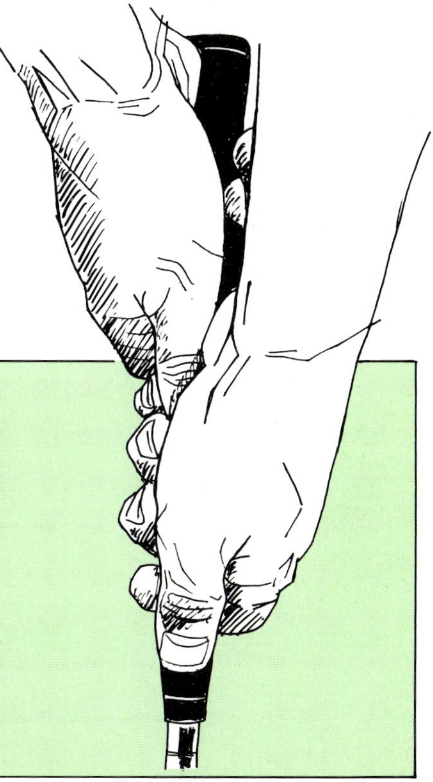

The type of grip often favoured by Bernhard Langer to prevent the dreaded 'yips' causing him problems on his short putts.

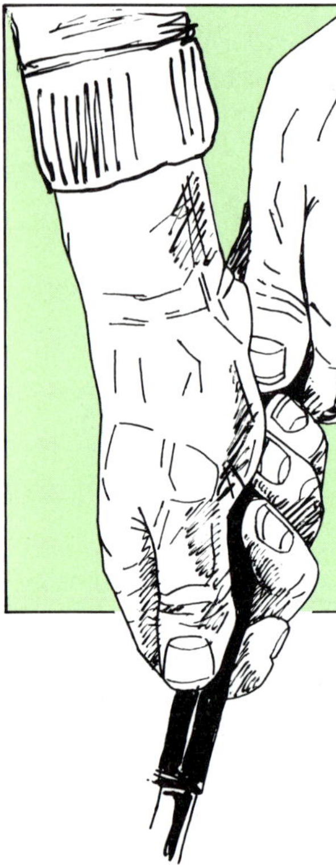

The hammer style putting grip which has all ten fingers on the handle and allows some golfers to use the same grip for putting as for hitting normal shots.

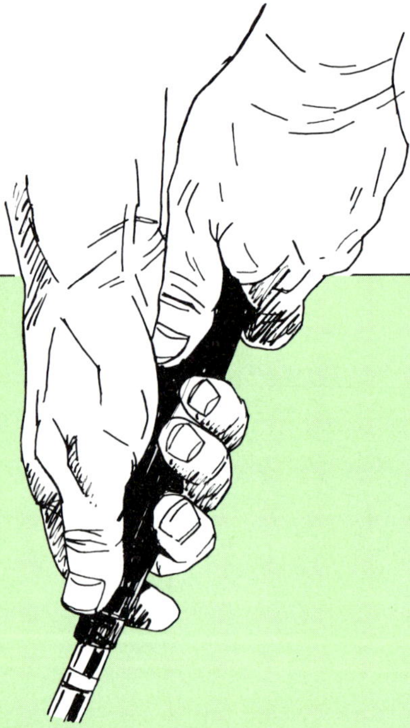

The split-handed grip with both thumbs on top of the grip, the hands apart and almost covering the whole length of the handle.

Helping hands

When it comes to building a sound grip, there are a couple of points that are worth remembering. When the left hand is placed on the handle the key fingers are the last three. They hold the club in position under the heel of the hand and ensure that the club stays firm throughout the swing.

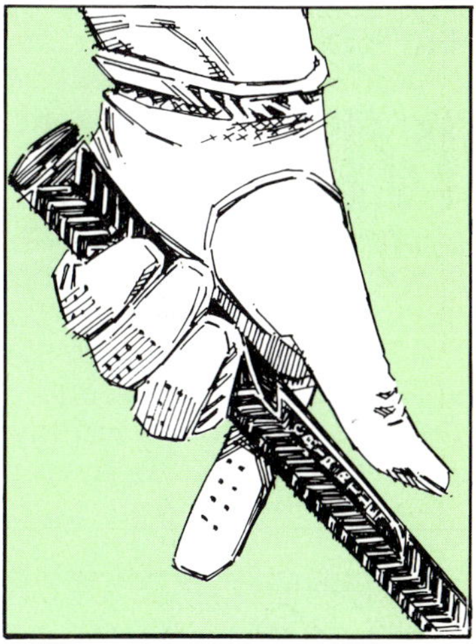

When the right hand is applied to the grip, it is the middle two fingers that play the most important role, as they help the last three fingers of the left hand maintain a firm grip.

The thumb and forefinger then fold around without either applying any real pressure to the grip.

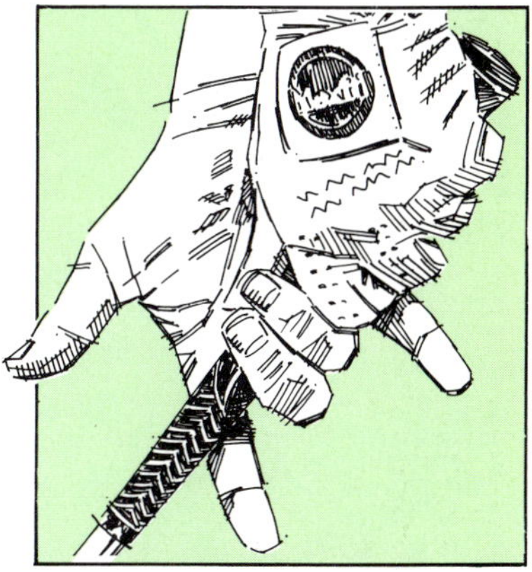

When the grip is completed, the V's formed between the index finger and thumb of both hands should point between your head and right shoulder in the case of a right handed player and vice versa for a leftie.

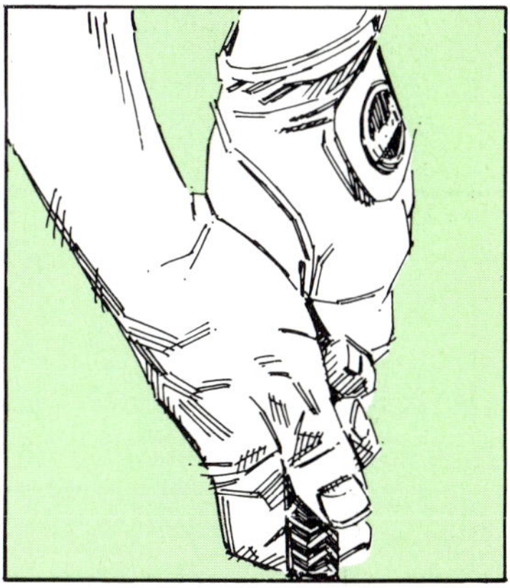

Grip tip

Many weekend golfers lose control of the club at the top of the backswing because they grip too close to the end of the handle. When the club is gripped in this way the left hand is unable to support it properly with the result that the club is allowed to move out of the correct plane.

So next time you take up your grip make sure there is at least an inch of the end of the club visible after you close your left hand around it. By doing this you will allow the heel of the palm to help support the weight of the club and give you better control.

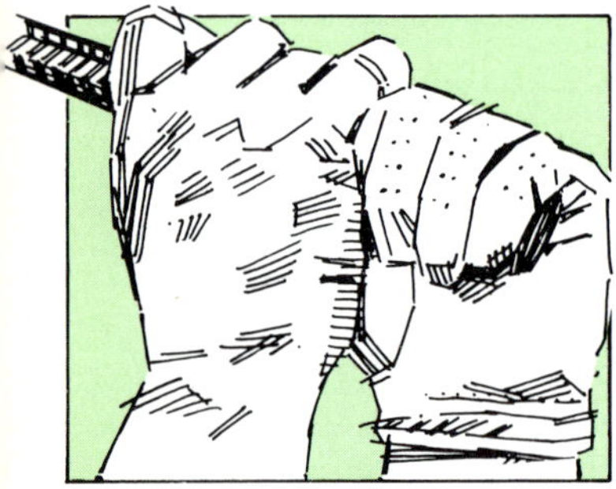

(Left) Gripping too close to the end of the handle. (Below) Gripping correctly.

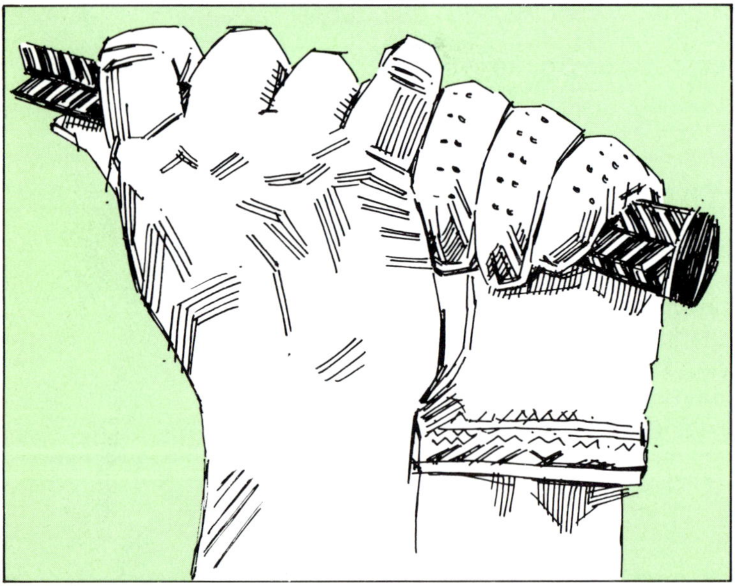

Grip check

The grip should always be checked as it is the basis of the swing. One simple way of checking your grip is to raise the club in front of your eyes and see if it is comfortable. If it is not, the grip is incorrect. It may be because your left hand is too far under the shaft. For the correct grip, the 'V' formed by the left thumb and forefinger points approximately to the right shoulder.

Now while you are holding the club in your left hand, place the right hand on the shaft, with the right thumb pressing over the left thumb. Try to keep the hands together so that they are kept in unison but do not grip tightly.

Raise the club in front of you holding it in your left hand and check if it is comfortable. Then bring your right hand onto the shaft.

CHAPTER 6

The rough

Wood from the rough

If you struggle getting out of the rough with your irons then why not try a 5 or 7 wood? The actual club you choose will depend on the distance you need to achieve and the lie of the ball.

For a bad lie in the rough make sure you position the ball back in your stance but keep your hands ahead of the ball with the back of the clubhead slightly raised above the ground.

Attempt to swing in a more upright plane to encourage a steeper angle of attack on the ball.

Feel as if you are chopping down more than sweeping away, as you would do from a good lie on the fairway with more of your weight on your left foot.

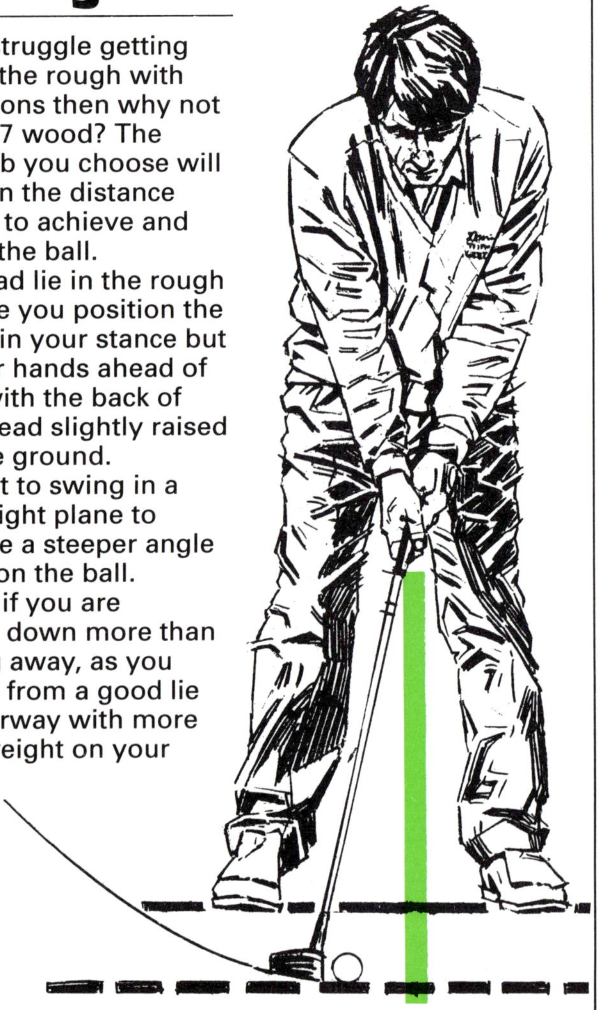

Rough justice

When playing from deep rough close the clubface slightly when addressing the ball. This compensates for the grass wrapping itself around the club as the shot is played and forcing the face open. It you address the shot with the clubface too open, this could lead to a shank.

Grip the club firmly, pick it up steeply in the backswing and swing down into the back of the ball. A full flowing follow-through is not required but try to keep the club going through after impact. Using a sand wedge gets the ball airborne quickly and the weight of the heavy flange will help drive the clubhead through the grass.

Be prepared to take your medicine and play out to a spot on the green, or a spot close to the green, instead of attempting the one-in-a-million shot.

Playing rough

Most golfers do not take enough care in selecting the right club when playing from the rough.

Club selection should be determined by the lie; even from quite deep rough, a long recovery shot is still possible, provided that you are lucky enough to find a good lie.

However, a bad lie in heavy rough is a very different proposition and leaves little alternative other than just to get the ball back into play. Avoid the temptation of trying to get too much distance from your recovery shot, especially if it will only mean the difference between hitting a 7 iron rather than a 6 for your third shot.

Instead, take the shortest and safest route back onto the fairway, using a club with which you feel confident of playing a successful recovery shot.

Taking the easy way out is as much for our mental as physical benefit. Trouble shots are the ones which eat away at our reserves of mental energy and whenever possible we should try to avoid these stress situations during a competitive round.

One way to help ease this mental stress is to practise playing recovery shots from all types of hazards. Drop a few balls in the rough and discover just how the ball reacts when you play a recovery shot with different clubs. This will help relieve some of the mental stress when you find yourself facing that same type of shot in a competitive round.

Tip from Brian Waites, Hollinwell GC, England

CHAPTER 7

Lies

Ball below your feet

When the ball is below the feet, the position of the ball in relation to the left heel along the line to the target does not change from that of a flat lie. What does change, however, is its distance from the front of you. If the ball has to be a little nearer you then shorten your grip on the club for an uphill lie and lengthen it for a downhill lie.

There is one simple way to make sure you have the ball positioned in the correct place. Take notice when you take your practice swing just where you make contact with the ground. The ball will then be positioned just behind this in relation to your feet.

Tip from Brian Waites, Hollinwell GC, England

Align your shoulders with the slope

If you tilt yourself to the right at address when you have a sloping lie, you will in effect give yourself a flat lie. The reason that this shot so often fails is that most golfers keep their shoulders level and then swing as they would for a normal lie. Align your shoulders with the slope and avoid swaying by restricting your body action on the backswing a little.

Use more armswing and less hip movement. The ball will fly higher and consequently you will get less distance, so club yourself accordingly. On a downhill lie the same principles apply but put more weight on your back foot. The ball will also fly lower and further than usual so when you choose your club, bear this in mind.

Sandy Lyle demonstrates perfect balance on this uphill shot.

Sloping lies

The position in which we place our feet in relation to the ball position is easy to work out when we have a flat lie. However, if the ball sits either higher or lower than our feet, then adjustments have to be made.

If you find yourself faced with a downhill lie, with your right foot higher than your left, then the ball should be positioned further back in the stance than normal. This will have the effect of changing your swing plane with the club travelling on a slightly out-to-in path which in turn will encourage the ball to slice or fade in flight.

As with an uphill lie, balance can be a problem, and in the case of downhill shots, loss of balance can sometimes lead to topped shots. This type of lie will also result in the ball flying on a lower trajectory, therefore less club will be required to cover the normal distance.

Tip from Brian Waites, professional, Hollinwell GC, England

CHAPTER 8

Around the green

Low flying wedge shot

To set up a low flying wedge shot which will stop quickly, play the ball well to the back of your stance.

Place your hands well ahead of the ball and make sure most of your weight is on your left side.

This will cause a steep downswing arc to give the low flight and backspin needed to stop the ball quickly.

Keep your hands well ahead of the clubhead through impact.

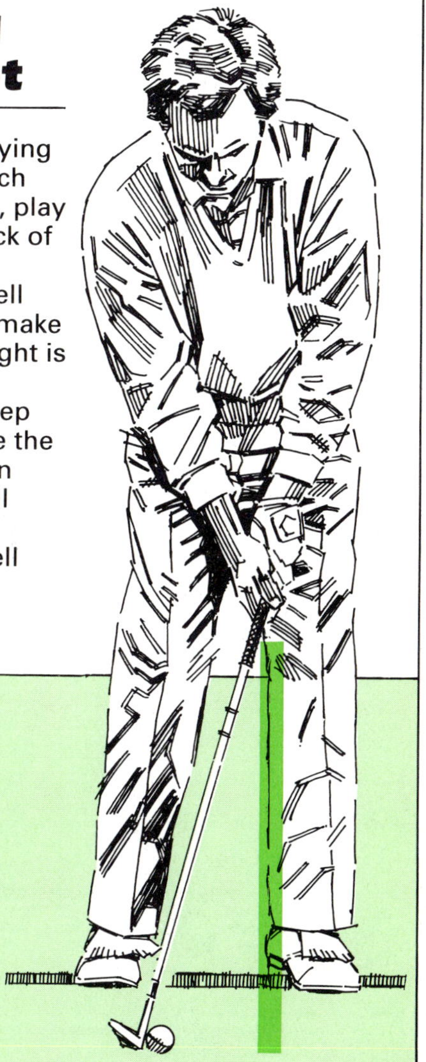

Quick Tips

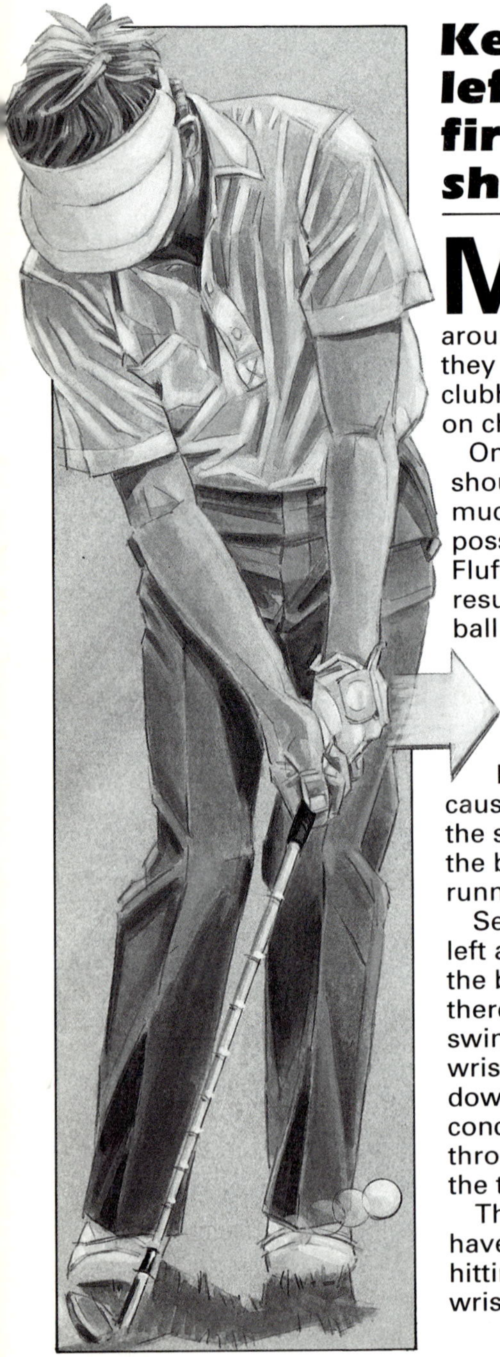

Keep the left wrist firm on chip shots

Many amateur golfers have a tough time around the greens because they try to flick the clubhead through the ball on chip shots.

On chip shots you should try to eliminate as much wrist action as possible from the stroke. Fluffed shots are the direct result of flicking at the ball with the wrists.

Excessive wrist action on the downstroke leads to fat chip shots, hitting the turf behind the ball. It also causes skulled shots, with the sole catching the top of the ball and sending it running across the green.

Set up with the weight left and the hands ahead of the ball, and keep them there throughout the swing. By keeping the left wrist firm on the downstroke you can simply concentrate on hitting through the ball towards the target.

The image you want to have is of the right hand hitting against the left wrist, not turning over it.

Chip and run

More often than not, you will be best advised to chip your ball short of the flag because with a short backswing, you will not be able to generate much backspin.

Look at the contours of the land to see where your ball will finish and how it will run on to the hole. Read the greens carefully for this feel shot.

This shot can be played with a straight-faced club although some golfers prefer to use a wedge and have their hands well forward of the club head.

It is essential to think positive with these shots and to visualise where the ball is going to land. As for all short shots around the green the swing does not reach more than waist height and it is essential to follow-through properly.

Aiming high

The easiest way to play a high shot is to open the club face and your stance which will cause the ball to rise quickly.

Play the ball a little further forward than you would for a normal shot and put more weight onto the right foot. Move your hands until they are level with the ball and allow the wrists to break early in the backswing.

Don't be short

We've all heard of the expression never up, never in. Usually it applies to the putting stroke, but most amateur players could do well to keep it in mind when playing chips shots.

More often than not the ball never gets up to the flag because high handicappers always want to play lofted chip shots from every conceivable spot around the green. However, even the smart players who play the sensible chip and run shots often have a tough time getting the ball close.

Most leave the ball well short of the hole because they are not confident enough when striking the ball. To be a good short game player you have to be aggressive enough to attack the flag. A tentative chipping stroke will only add shots to your score.

Here's a good tip to remember if you are consistently leaving the ball short. Disregard the flag altogether and imagine another flag two or three feet past the hole and aim at that spot. That way if you are leaving them short you will more than likely end up close to the hole.

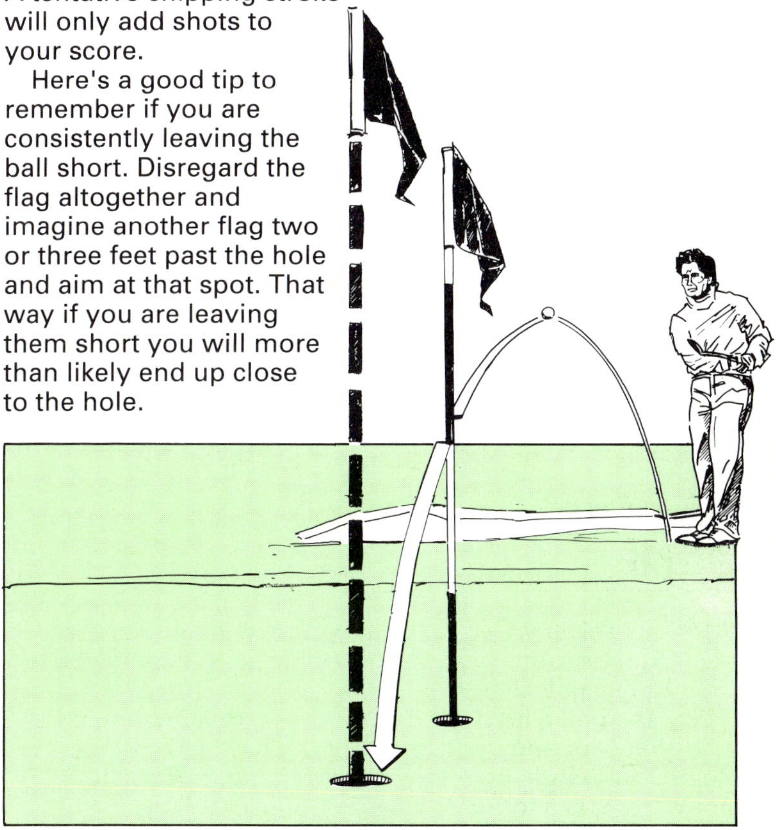

CHAPTER 9

The green

Putting single handed

To improve your short and middle range putting, practise holding the club in your left hand only. Line up your putt as normal with both hands on the grip but just before you start your stroke, take your right hand off the grip (let it hang free or put it in your pocket). Then go ahead and strike the putt as normal.

This may help ensure you keep the putter head acceleration on through the ball and also to prevent the right hand taking over and turning the face of the putter to the left.

Long and medium range putts

If you find that you are having difficulty getting up to the hole on medium and long range putts, check that you don't have the ball positioned too far back in your stance.

If the ball is too far back, the hands may get ahead at address and this can lead to a downward strike on the ball producing backspin and causing the ball to stop quicker than you might anticipate.

If the ball is positioned further forward in the stance, with the hands above or even slightly behind the ball, it is more likely that the putter will strike the ball on the upswing, imparting overspin and making it run further.

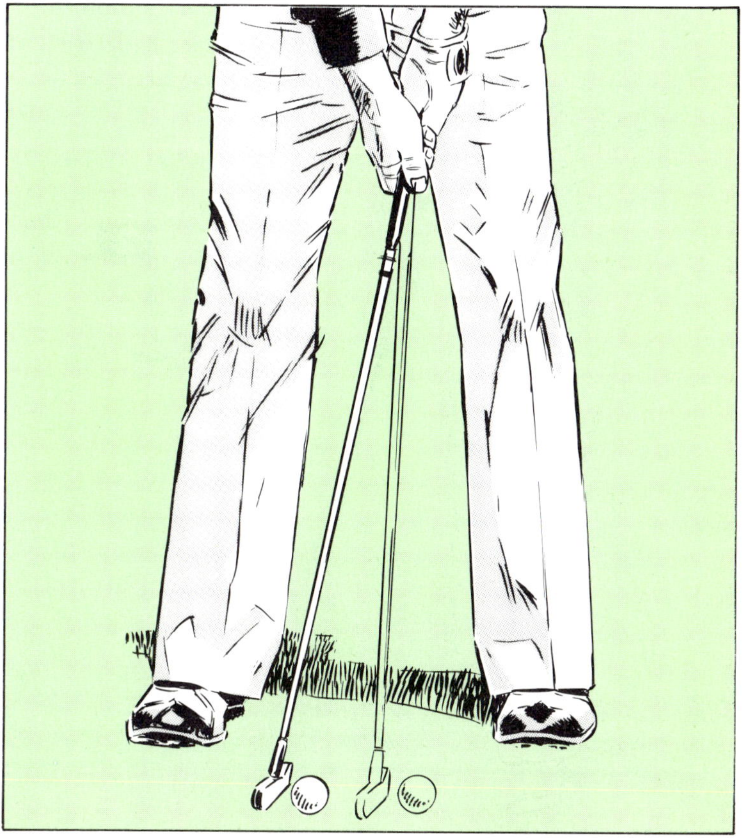

Judging the speed of a putt

You can learn something about the pace of your putt simply by studying the putting surface. Look at the striped patterns left by the mower. The darker strip is cut against the grain and the lighter strip is cut with the grain.

The darker strip grass will be standing more upright and will provide more resistance to the ball. On the other hand the lighter grass is lying flatter which will allow the ball to run with less resistance, producing a faster putt.

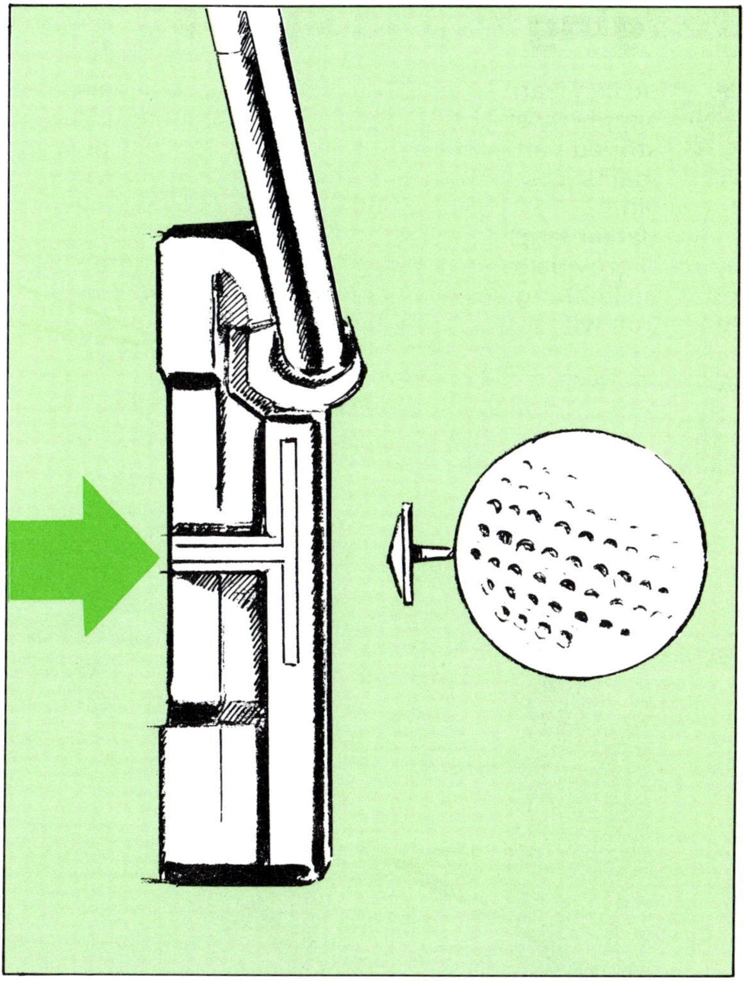

Curing tentative short putting

If you are having trouble with three to four feet putts you may find the following tip useful. Try to imagine that there is a tack sticking into the back of the ball and that you are attempting to tap the tack into the ball with your putter, instead of making an ineffectual stroking action. This can be especially effective on bumpy winter greens.

Putting on the up

If your putting is on perfect line but is stopping six inches short of the hole, resist the temptation to condemn your putter to the darkest corner of the attack and to try a new one.

The set-up may be to blame. If the ball is hit with the putter moving slightly on the downswing, a certain amount of backspin is imparted so that it will sometimes actually check, or skid slightly before it begins to roll. It may not travel as far as you anticipated.

However when the ball is struck slightly on the upswing, overspin is created and the ball tends to run a little more smoothly and travels further. By moving the ball towards your left foot you will be able to strike the ball slightly on the upswing.

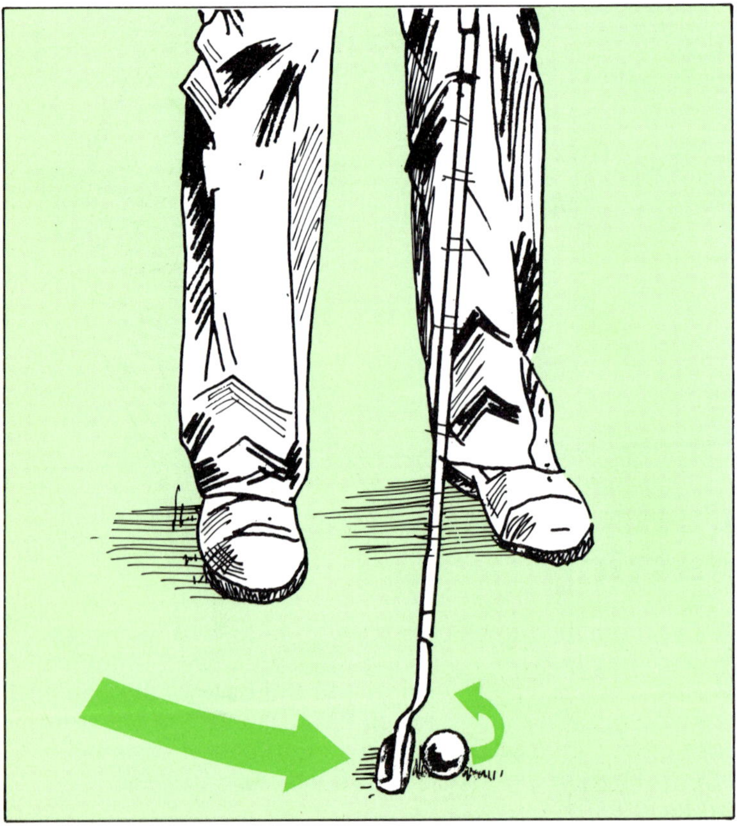

Get on the right path

If you are missing five and six foot putts regularly to the right, check that you are in fact taking the putter back in a straight line and not fanning the club open in the backswing. This is an exercise you can try at home that will help solve the problem.

Take your normal putting stance with the putter's toe as close as possible to the skirting board that runs along the bottom of a wall. Then simply swing the putter back and forth, for the appropriate distance required. You can now see if the club face is fanning open and if you are taking the club back too much on the inside.

CHAPTER 10

Left-handers

Tips from John Nolan, professional, Cavendish GC, England

Back to basics

If you talk to left-handed golfers, most feel aggrieved at the lack of teaching manuals for them. But is this really a problem? Many left-handers find it better to learn from a right-handed professional.

The golf swing is the same no matter whether you're right-handed or left-handed. When a right-hander demonstrates the grip and set-up to left-handed pupils, they can see a mirror image of their own grip. Right-handers should benefit in this way when being taught by left-handed professionals.

As in the case of a right-handed player, left-handers should ensure that the club sits in the fingers of both hands and not in the palms. You should be able to see two or three knuckles on the right hand. The Vs created by the thumb and forefinger of each hands should point to the left shoulder. Don't make the mistake of holding the club too tightly in the left hand as this will take the feel out of the shot.

Positional play

Finding the correct ball position is just as difficult for a left-hander as it is for the right-hander. Often an inch or two can mean the difference between hitting the putting surface or being in the bunker.

Set up for most shots with the ball just inside your right foot. This ensures that your right arm and club are in a straight line down to the ball. By adopting this address position, you can guarantee that your hands are slightly ahead of the ball, which is when striking the ball.

Setting up with the right arm and club in line has another benefit: it means that the right shoulder is higher than the left shoulder at address, the way it should be for southpaws. This set-up also promotes a smooth, one-piece take-away from the ball.

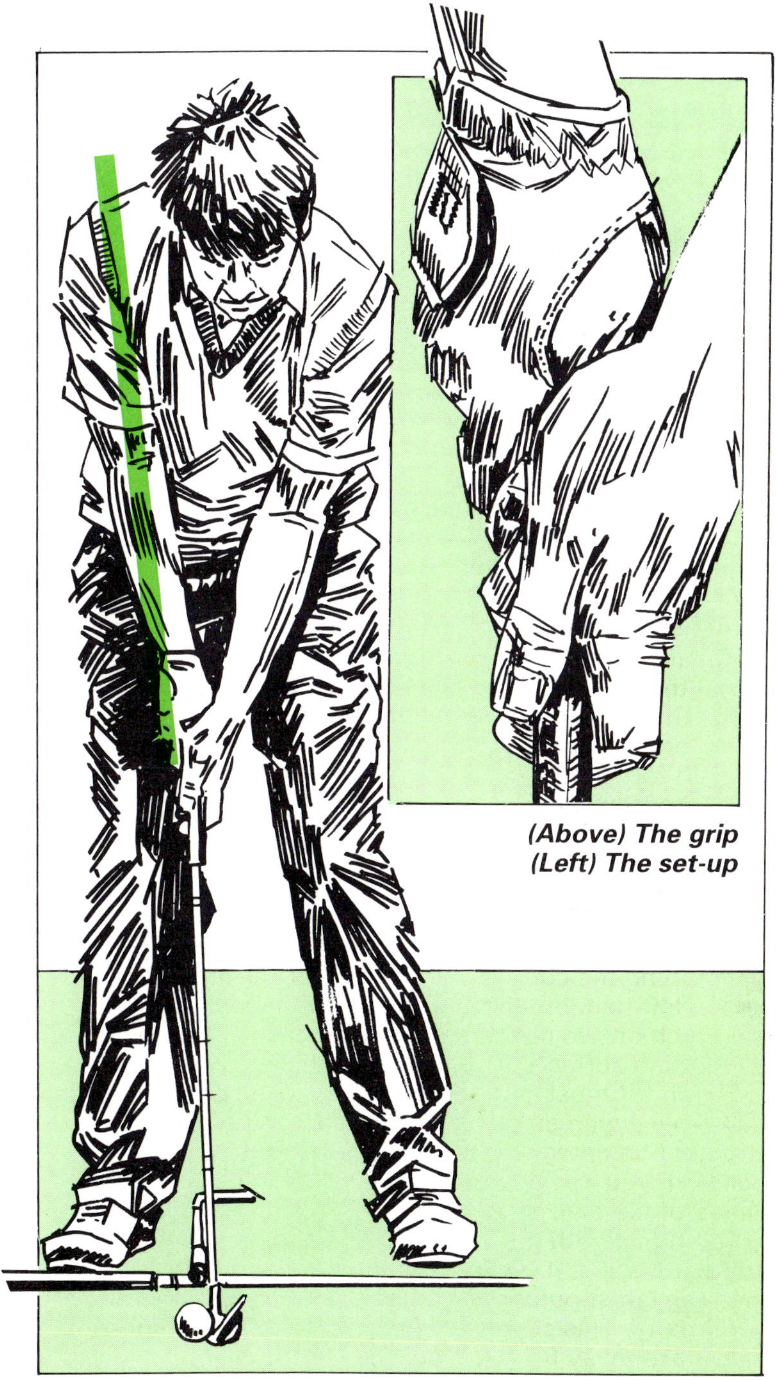

(Above) The grip
(Left) The set-up

Quick Tips

Left isn't always right for the lefties

Many left-handed golfers suffer because they let the left side take over in the backswing. They find it difficult to accept the fact that the right side, the weaker side, is the dominating side in the swing for a left-hander.

Two problems can result when a southpaw player lets the left side take over the swing: firstly, the club is picked up abruptly by the left hand which causes it to start back outside the line (below right); or, secondly, it is pulled too far inside the line (below left) to allow the player to make a proper backswing.

What the left-handed player has to work on is taking the club away from the ball correctly at the beginning of the swing. The most effective way to do this is to push the club back from the ball in a one-piece motion at the beginning of the backswing (right). To facilitate this, the leftie has to hand over control to the right side.

By pushing the club back with the right hand and arm, the left-hander will guarantee that the club starts on the

proper path. Then it is just a matter of allowing the body to turn naturally to complete the backswing.

Work on controlling the swing with the right side and you will develop a swing that starts back naturally from the ball; your swing will also have a better chance of staying on line.

Quick Tips

Left in line

Posture is just as important for left-handed players as it is for right-handers. When setting up, ensure that everything is parallel to the target line — shoulders, hips, knees, feet and eyes. Adopt a relaxed posture and be sure to let the arms hang freely to allow them to swing unimpaired.

The left shoulder is a big problem for left-handers. Because it is the stronger side, there is a tendency for the left-shoulder to take over the swing. Usually it moves out and opens up the shoulders so that the body is aiming right of the target, thereby causing the player to pull across the ball.

One key to keeping the shoulders swinging on line is to tuck in the left elbow at address. This keeps the left shoulder below the right as it should be and lets the shoulders turn on the proper axis.

Lead with the right arm

Once the downswing has begun and the left hander has handed over control to the right side of the body, it is vital to maintain right side control.

It is important that the power generated by the right side in the downswing does not disappear either by letting the left arm and shoulder get into the act or by unlocking the wrists too early.

The first fault should not happen provided that the right side has taken over full control and passed it on to the right arm in the downswing. After the hips have turned back towards target, the right arm then pulls the clubhead down into the ball.

Notice how in the illustration the right arm is pulling the club down into the ball and the relationship between the club shaft and the right arm has remained the same as it was at the top of the backswing. If you uncock the wrists too early, all the power generated by the body and the pulling action of the right side will be ruined.

Once the downswing has started you should concentrate on pulling the club down and through the ball with the right arm. Don't uncock the wrists too early in the swing. You should not be thinking of uncocking the wrists until the hands reach belt buckle level. Uncocking the wrists should be the final stage of the downswing, transmitting the energy generated by the right side and arm into the back of the ball.

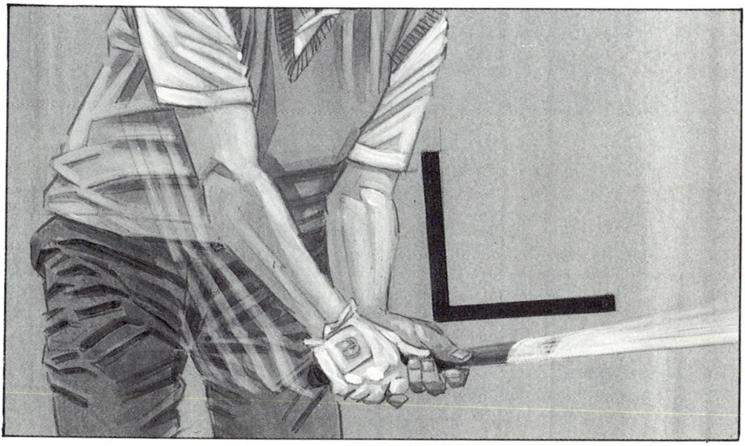

Think right from the top

The first impulse that a left-handed player has at the top of the swing is to throw the club with the dominant left side. This is a very natural impulse, but unfortunately it is not the one that will lead to good golf.

A good backswing will leave the hips turned half as much as the shoulders, which should be at 90 degrees with the back facing the target. At this point all the left-hander has to do is succumb to the right side, especially the right hip. The proper turn creates tension between the shoulders and the hips, which will have naturally resisted the shoulders during the backswing.

To use the power created by the coil between the hips and shoulders, let the right side pull your body through to the target naturally. The right hip will turn towards the target and then it is only a matter of pulling through with your right arm and side.

This will ensure that the club approaches from the proper angle and that the weight is transferred to the right foot.